About the Author

A father of four, artist, and poet from Anderson, SC who has finally completed the dream of writing his second book.

Love, Lust and Romanticism

Slongentl, and Da Reaper

Love, Lust and Romanticism

Olympia Publishers
London

www.olympiapublishers.com
OLYMPIA PAPERBACK EDITION

Copyright © Slongentl, and Da Reaper 2024

The right of Slongentl, and Da Reaper to be identified as author of this work has been asserted in accordance with sections 77 and 78 of the Copyright, Designs and Patents Act 1988.

All Rights Reserved

No reproduction, copy or transmission of this publication may be made without written permission.
No paragraph of this publication may be reproduced, copied or transmitted save with the written permission of the publisher, or in accordance with the provisions
of the Copyright Act 1956 (as amended).

Any person who commits any unauthorised act in relation to this publication may be liable to criminal prosecution and civil claims for damage.

A CIP catalogue record for this title is available from the British Library.

ISBN: 978-1-80439-536-3

This is a work of fiction.
Names, characters, places and incidents originate from the writer's imagination. Any resemblance to actual persons, living or dead, is purely coincidental.

First Published in 2024

Olympia Publishers
Tallis House
2 Tallis Street
London
EC4Y 0AB

Printed in Great Britain

Dedication

I dedicate this book to dreams of hard work paying off coming true.

Acknowledgements

A special thank you to everyone that has been supportive of my journey and growth as a poet.

I Want A Woman

I want a woman like…
Morning baby
As her head disappears for
A li'l morning ecstasy
I want a woman like…
Dressed up in an Eagle's jersey
Face painted along with nails
To express that she loved me
Wanting to be a part of my sports
Damn… she got me
After a long stressful day
Bath drawn
Dinner cooked
Her as dessert
On the counter she lay
Long massages heated foreplay
As we discuss the future
That we want to make
Her career mesh with mine
Together we will be
"One Band…One Sound"
I want a woman like…
Holds me close
As I shed tears at times
For we all know

The world gets cruel
When you are down sometimes
Help me catch my breath
When I'm all bent out of shape
Put another woman in her place
Without grasping her nape
I want a woman who
Never puts down my dreams
But incorporates herself in each and every scene
I want a woman
So beautiful
So true
Look deep within thyself
Maybe that woman is YOU

Thoughts Of You

in time I freeze
for at instant's glance
I see thee
beautiful as glory itself
a stature fused with heavenly wealth
every avenue taken to avoid capture
synchronized in loves embrace
in every inch of thy loving face
may I cuddle with the thoughts
of thee and I
unified at the thighs
eyes fixated yet mesmerized
will you take me to that special place
enduring the most sensual race
going at an unprecedented pace
soften kisses uniquely placed
be my queen each and every day

Look For Me

look for me
in your heart
and it's there that
you will find me

wrap your heart around me
make me
your whole life

if my heart was my arms
I would wrap them
around your soul forevermore

swept up in your arms
I wish to forever be
me loving you
you loving me

Start Or Seven Years

my world paused as we first glanced
knees buckled as you walked near
never knew beauty could be shaped so clear
crystalized in erotic form
yearning to have you
under my arms
could love overshadow
our lusty alarms
didn't want to risk this opportunity
with a tired pick-up line
so quietly I watch as you
offered the first line
after this line we started
the first day of seven years
some filled with ecstasy
some filled with tears
we have mourned
we have sensually joined
no one can ever compare
to the love in which ignites our air
passion never matched
in each other's hearts our
names forever patched
strictly together with Cupid's thread
intertwined divine

our hearts
our heads
immortality our fate
whether they love or hate
just let us be
alone long enough
to be a unity
matrimony you and I
just say the words
and I too
I do

Your Insecurities Don't Dictate Me

why must everyday
seem like my love
grows further away
divided by the very sense of us

strength now cannot
carry loads of a bus
push face first in life's pile of shit
I'm about ready to say fuck all this

your insecurities don't dictate me
it's your choice
stay
or be free

I pick me over you
is the words you said
sounds selfish that a motherfucker
when it's you instead

my life became our life
our life was their life
their life is dying
through our strife

Charlie

agony swells its overwhelming muscles
harmful yet tender thoughts
of you loving me all through the night
haunting my horniest dreams
I punch myself in the gut so
that yearns yield not for you
may another come and push me
past your pleasures beyond to
a realm never experienced
my mind body and soul take
ecstasy's hand without your guide
as I watch her sleep
I take a look at her caller id as
her phone rings aggressively
as my eyes widen fast
taken back to hours' past
she vanishes without a trace
reappearing at his place
karma has come full circle
for she is his who
nestles under the covers
as light glows around me
as an angel's birth
he is about to see all he's worth
a veil has been taken off my eyes

finally, I realize
we have switched souls deep inside
for I am he
and he is I...
Charlie

Amidst The Pain...The Struggle

Anger fills my bloodied muscle
Amidst the pain...the struggle
Discovering not all pieces fit to our puzzle
How can a conversation take part of my soul away
Guess I was never loved in the first place
I brought this all on myself
For being a real ass motherfucker when no one else
Has been that open book
There were so many chances
Most overlooked
It's now too late done cast thy hook
Into waters unknown for goodness' sake
Laying at the bottom of Lovers Lake
Creepin' I think was a big mistake
I placed in you something good
That no one else has in thy hood
For granted this all was taken
For it was in her pussy that I dipped in
Slowly our trust was shaken
Couldn't relax had to check
Messages, phones, and mail at that
From here nor there
Did I reign supreme
Just wanted love
Not a one-sided fling

This is what I live with day to day
Wondering
How can a conversation take part of my soul away

May I Encase Your Love

May we be that never ending love story
I envisioned since my eyes first laid sight of you as they
Encase every morsel feeling
Your body language spoke to them
Love letters forever yearning

May I take the pages forever turning as
I grovel in the thought of us
Encase the moment of passion and lust
Your mental stimulation clinches to me
Love you tender just let me please with all sincerity…

May I Encase Your Love?

please give clarity!

Cherry Blossoms

daybreak showers fall
along the sides of autumn
perpendicular

our lips sealed tightly
bodies loosening also
its ants in our pants

dramatic the scene
cherry blossoms opening
we were one tonight

Ode To Self

an ode to myself
sending a dove's tear-filled eye
eternally gone

all hopes devoured
flowers resume death by love
never live again

unopen thy heart
fill it till the waters bring
encased air unbreathed

perform mouth to mouth
so I can breathe once again
green leaves fall slowly

Tsunami Of Her

from within the underbelly of the Atlantic
I snivel
waves of lusty water
filled with a mélange of fish
unequaled to convey this lonesome hardship
arctic chills syringed throughout my pacific tide
heartbroken tips of the iceberg
plunge ungratefully slow
transforming into spongy algae
around my dead-beat heart
memoirs of history shed
the tsunami of her wreckage
I ache therefore
I'm healed through her...
the ocean

Rapture

yes the end is near
and all you got left now is
memories of us

memories of us
stuck between thy pearly gates
yes the end is near

yes the end is near
we gather here to be wed
memories of us

memories of us
at the alter we accept
the end is near

the end is near
please take us up in the air
memories of us

memories of us
finally the end is here
it is the rapture

Fade To Black

there is a flame that burns inside
but not for me its heat reside
I sit and watch you yearn all right
every time we argue and fight
yeah it's a fire of pain
painful jealousy and questions untamed
the blood drops used as toyous play
I found you in the toilet today
who but me lifts you in his arms
carries you to safety away from harm
you have burdens
shit me too
does anyone attempt to help me get through
I have said plenty but you
did not hear
guess it wasn't important enough
to unplug your ears
tears form and swell your eyes
for the world to see
my heart pumps tears
no one cares but me
as you fade to black
I cry not
for this whole time
I've stretched out my arms for you

to save you from your pain
you stare a blank stare never to return again

Long Nights...Short Days

every thought of you enrages me
how could you just release me
no heart no feeling... I'm beneath thee
but I'm the one who held you down wholeheartedly

passion kissed explosive orgasms
never knew it wasn't all that we could fathom
one night without warnings to tell
I'm out he's in...a bitter farewell

long nights...short days I thought of you
tricking myself into that's what you wanted to do
I realized that was not the case
that day I seen you face to face

you feel me deeply more than physical
exhaling every chance we are together at will
holding me close...releasing me tight
one day we will be together...everything's right

Matrimonial Intertwined

life could not get any more complete
a little you and a little me
together forever…
eternity
I have held you in my arms
many times it's different now
since we are matrimonial intertwined
our eyes see a little deeper within our flow
embraces filled with unfathomed love
I will take my shirt off to shelter you from rain
if it means that it will also heal your pain
I'm here at times when you need release
just lie on your stomach
your stress my hands will take care of it
when sickness overcomes your means
baby I am all your antihistamines
for I will touch your soul at depths never noticed
always I'm here to help get us focused
that throbbing you get between your thighs
my tongue will take you from the ground up into ecstasy's sky
my stroke will bring shortness of breath felt in the womb
don't worry just hold me all of it consume
when you need a shoulder
I will be your boulder
all you ever could want and more
I'll be all you need as we together grow older

Finally Slongentl

many moons from now
I envision
a splice between you and I
how I will take others
into my bedroom
you will receive all you can to replace me...
that very best man
eggshells that you carelessly tracked upon
hopelessly cracked with stupidity
here I am released from
all this tension
mentioning times ancient to now
when lovers made unknown how
between fiery sheets we did lay
warm mornings awakened with
sensual sensitivity laid out
upon a platter...
strawberries
peaches
whip cream
delicious were you
memories now whitened out
driven by
promiscuous passions
finally...
I am Slongentl

SLONGENTL

Saturating pulpy sensations
Lingering mentally inside
One's sensual persona
Negotiating the art of lovemaking
Gently as the sun goes down until
Eventually I rise to cater to your muse
Nymphomaniacally reimbursing the thrusting
Till all is emptied
Labeled as The King Of Erotica

It's not only a word but a way of life…
As the ladies moan SLONGENTL

Slo's Attraction

I am...thy interest...
The law of physical attraction
Bumps on thy arm
Wetness opposite of the norm
Sounding the alarm
Warning you
Darling you falling yet standing
For me many degrees burn beneath thy navel
Consent me to embellish the meal
Exhale while your pupils dilate
Inhale while my tongue reciprocates the wave
As you flirt atop the crest of me
Slo...n...Gently...no gravity
It's tempting to open thy eyes
don't
Explore the beauty of seduction's confidence
Licking...sucking...temptation
Depleting....retreating
From me
as our scent rise as the sun
We connect till the setting is done
There is no escape you are captive
Explicitly experiencing essential ecstasy
Magnetism to the fourth degree
As many times you can

I decree
I inhale you
You exhale me
We are one
Heartbeat
Please allow me to be
YOUR FANTASY

Eyes Blue As The Softest Sea

eyes blue as the softest sea
love's addiction got a hold on me
control me gently in the palm of thy tongue
drank me thirstily like an aged shot of rum

squeezing tighter than the mightiest grip
drank me thirstily like an aged shot of rum
climaxing free as a summer's breeze
love's addiction got a hold on me

control me gently in the palm of thy tongue
hurry please get thy bra undone
eyes blue as the softest sea
floating around in ecstasy

licking my way through the ABCs
floating around in ecstasy
using calligraphy at X, Y, and Z
climaxing free as a summer's breeze

hurry please get thy bra undone
panties too as I fondle thy buns
squeezing tighter than the mightiest grip
lets not forget the handcuffs and whips

Divinely Placed

unique skyline beach front property
lights music cue open sesame
bodies reeling faster and faster still
breathing heavenly feelings touché
outlawed actions brilliantly performed
divinely placed in each other's arms
exotic synergy erogenous zones
ecstatic energy spent all gone

Interior Decorate

may I interior decorate
the inside of your walls
form a chemistry between
my paint and your sheetrock
may I turn the knob on your oven
to heat things up a bit
I beg to lay out your futon
and test thy springs
I'm gonna use different wattage
for your lights are not as bright as I like
maybe a twist or two will do the trick
pull and twist to get the shower going
is it comfortable in your hands
no…
then let me continue
to knock all your picture frames into place
one hard shift at a time
before I leave
I must put my special cleaner
onto your floor
so it will gleam with shine
happiness will swim across thy face
as a handsome check you shall write
for my services were well worth the price

Painting

for humanity to behold our portrait personified
one must exhibit the debonair evanescence of art
colors sublime
mélange with that breathtaking aura thy paint possess
by splurging onto the soft silken canvas provided
ready openly to begin the stroke
strong statured brush awaiting thy command
which will mix the mother of all mixtures
to hang my masterpiece
on thy uninhabited gallery walls for this is
the core of my creativity

Sexual Graffiti

let me speak
my sensuality
better yet
allow me
to lick my
sexual graffiti
all over your
vaginal walls
my signature style
world renown
erotically I airbrush the scene
tantric techniques
until commanded by thee
to release the flood
thy face serves
as our second canvas
a creamy watercolor
forms a facemask
refining
smiling as you take my brush
pull and squeeze determined
to empty thy lust
to make a color
unknown to man
allowing me to create

a legendary masterpiece
the gallery's showcase
when two souls' kinetic energy
collide taste to taste

Open Sesame

honey I'm home
open sesame
constantly palpitating
gyrating collaboration
including fingertips upon recollecting
toothsome scenes
backwards is time
liquid filled testes
throb with anticipation
all is stupendous
with little negotiation
titillating in innumerable positions
you fix ones gaze in awe
in every way we lay
as I coagulate inside
you constrict around me
a movie could not ensnare
a more perfect episode
both taken captive in passion's bliss
owned by each other's innards
which outwardly set us free
so unconscious to sensual consciousness
that revival would be revelation
bodies wail out in ecstasy
while whispering rapture

all night long
so wrenching wet
so intensely broiling
honey I'm home
open sesame

Episodes Slowed

episodes slowed perfectly scripted
international lover legs exquisitely lifted
wet to gush intensity grows
slippery to squirt ecstasy knows

international lover legs exquisitely lifted
long deep and hard vigorously gifted
tight grip loose lips skillfully shows
wet to gush intensity grows

yearning initiates moans as clothes sifted
episodes slowed perfectly scripted
slippery to squirt ecstasy knows
juices and spasms create creamy flows

long deep and hard vigorously gifted
toes curled to the max release is eminent
seeping tastefully cumming gracefully
tight grip loose lips skillfully shows

talking dirty heightens pleasure
tongue traveling through thy sensual treasure
to the victor goes the spoils
showered entirely with bodily oils

To Do List

I see those eyes
not filled with pride
overflowing with someone else's compromise
for thee I despise
since the love here is waiting patiently
the signs it seems you're not getting lately
we embrace in empty salutations
for there is no one else for me but you
as I reach the bottom of you
you will see plainly
or shall I say feel my depth for you
receive my warmth
it melts within thy grasp
overflowing with mini feelings of passion
eagerly awaiting to weld within you
it seems like forever as I
slowly pull outward from thee
you stop
grab my ass and whisper
please baby inside of me
I continue to dream of this day
we explore this bliss
equally anticipating
crossing each other off our
to do list

Spit Persona

Thought I would hit the ladies with a li'l alter ego erotic conversation hope you enjoy

**notice the lady in that long red dress
I am positive she can handle the best
which is me Mr. Slongentl
guaranteed to sexually set her free**

oh shorty in da red ain't thinking bout you
she see this ten inch dick and don't know what to do
wondering how she can take it deeper
she's heard that they call me the Da Reaper

**what do you know about pleasing a woman
massage therapy with a li'l tonguing
feeding her peaches, cream, and strawberries too
put my face all up in her if she wants me to**

don't know nothing 'bout pleasing
but well advanced in swelling pussy up
bang bang bang till she can't get up
to the back and then some down her throat

**candles, wine, a movie or two
a hot steamy bath in the jacuzzi is how I do
carrying her through rose petals to the bed**

**making love till morning shed
that's me Slongentl in the flesh**

lights off, a porno, a beer or two
I took a bath before I came and she did too
bending her over right here on the bar
when she has finished cumming
her mind for sure gone off
won't be back till morning come
now swimming in the head of her
what Da Reaper has done

**well let's flip for her to see who win
damn… tails, I lose again
don't worry I might need your help if it get out of hand
yeah I know I'm the closure of the land**

Centerfold

midnight strikes the dawn of a new day
the pavilion on the scene of hips
swaying to and fro each and every way
sweet tension of seduction perfumes the air
million dollar boxer briefs
shed at the "get together" under the reef
I can sense in her eyes
lonely as can be
in her mansion
her secrets are safe with me
her evasion of him
is fine by me
the crime
she's married
and getting beat by he
I came through
laid it down thoroughly
I feel it in my heart
my actions are cold
but what's a man to do
when she's a centerfold

No Pulling Out To The Call Of No Return

splash goes the elongated thrill
through rapids so roughly evenly still
sticky but slippery nipple to feel
gasping searching for ecstasy's quill

dead
whiffle ball's whisper to the call of no return
dead man's rise to the undertaker's demise
hell fire and brimstone ashes smolder

deeper…deeper…deeper…till
waterbed imploding from within she will
splash goes the elongated thrill
sticky but slippery nipple to feel

apparition's vision blurred clear as day
trick by life's magician goes magnificently
souls gone evermore to arrive once more
finality infinitely imprinted indefinitely

waterbed imploding from within she will
as a flickered light goes on and off
deeper…deeper…deeper…till
eyes roll ragefully soft

hell fire and brimstone ashes smolder
dead man's rise to the undertaker's demise
whiffle ball's whisper to the call of no return
dead

higher the sensation above the loft
shoving it harder resisting at all cost
short bursts of quivering shakingly ecstatic
no pulling out slow motion is romantic

In My Sanctuary

come my dear
to my sanctuary
here I will cleanse you
of the mess you have made
I will eradicate all misfortunes
intentional or not done unto your body
I shall heal every nook and cranny of your being
be one with me
one in whom sacrificing
your former self will be done
afterwards you will be
fresh and anew
a whole other era
will disperse from your soul
Slongentl will be the flow
of each pop and lock
deep kneading penetration
as if undergoing massage therapy
manage a trois therapy would be more suffice
you can taste her while
she laps you
I shall spank the both of you
I feel the moistened tunnels constricting
upon my fingertips
as you beg me to unfold destiny's plan
upon the release on those beautiful lips

Perpetrating As Love's Ambassador

perpetrating as love's ambassador
may I enter you fully
to give lessons that rimfully set her
heart at ease her knight crowned king

to give lessons that rimfully set her
soul on fire erotically exploding
insides deteriorated to and implosion of him
perpetrating as love's ambassador

insides deteriorated to and implosion of him
sensing the hunger in the lioness's eyes
mood encrypted enchantment inside
to give lessons that rimfully set her

exquisitely satisfied from head to toe
heart at ease her knight crowned king
may I enter you fully
for it is eating me within

unsheathe me to the gleeful end
perpetrating as love's ambassador
soul on fire erotically exploding
the luxury of having our love unloading

seduction marked as passion is felt
to give lessons that rimfully set her
sensing the hunger in the lioness's eyes
forcing me to conquer her with a lion's pride

perpetrating as love's ambassador
to give lessons that rimfully set her
insides deteriorated to and implosion of him
exquisitely satisfied from head to toe

Enwrapped By Me

seizing the moment
at its immaculate manifestation
a platform esteemed
above the norm
encoded with a code
all its own
as you solicit me
to reapply myself
you compress
I swell heavily deep
within thy moistened sleeve
shaven like a suburban lawn
every follicle tastefully detached
my mind encases yours
as we fervently attach
pelvic thrusts sequenced
on autopilot
steam arise
as you proceed to get dug out
by the love juggernaut
sweet genie of lover's hope
may thee ice liquify down thy slope
as I haul it out
no laugh
no joke

only for thee to put it back
in its original stroke
feigning for my brick
of dope
as your climax near
appears that you are
strangling yourself
without any rope
our demeanors calm
enough so you insist
on sleeping in my arms
placid shall be tonight
you allowed your soul
to be enwrapped by me
our essence of lovemaking
enchanted by we

Intimate Entity

an intimate entity
heard deep off beyond the soul
sensual enigma unveiled
title of "super lover" held
tight as the weld of lust inside
increasing the intensity orally abiding
moan so loud its volumeless
so big it fills thy emptiness
extra wet
extra creamy
tasting it
leaving you dreamy
as you begin the ascension
into ecstasy's heaven
angelic like whispers of affection
reacquaint themselves with my ears
realm of satisfaction moves us to tears
as we embrace sensual matrimony
climaxed as the world turns
simmering as we rock each other sleepily
only to awaken to the dawn of a new day
refreshed and anxious to rekindle
the night before our flesh meshed
into momentary unconsciousness

Sentimental Sapphires

sentimental sapphires glow evanescently
on thy neck and fingers
the scent of Chanel on thy breast
still lingers
lungs heavily ingest thy fragrance
intake like a sole hand of solitaire
each card awaits its destination
every flip a chance to make a move
smoothly as thy lips began to moisten
you want it now and often
saturation too much to bear
assisting you orally to ease thy fear
of me hurting what's beating inside
I assure you there's nothing to hide
apologetic stares for I am about to
put it on you
own you
as I stamp my trojans inside of you
throwing it back
and I'm giving it all to you
up and down
like the graph on a heart monitor
in this ring
I'm the matador
coming to eradicate all disbelief

destressing thy meaty reef
as thy insides massage my thickened beef
transforming fantasies into erotic truths
blues nevermore
at the receiving end of phone calls galore
the more we explore
becomes the best
you ever had before

Sensual Asteroids

my mind bends in uncanny positions
as I orbit her earth
sensually her planet flourish
with life everlasting
each star erogenously zoned
so that they sparkle
when reached well
within their limits
my rocket releases itself
into her sky
sprinkling sensual asteroids
as it explodes
reaching altitudes so great
changing her sun into her moon
simultaneously with each climax
overflowing her galaxy with
remembrance of ecstasy's reign

Intimacy Of Mind And Pen

you dream of world unveiled
as the heavens itself conjure its tale
reminiscent of times afar
life goes on
my soul an open jar
expression is a poet's outlet
assuring you I can't live without it
different meanings for different phases
awkward stares and distant gazes
no one understand me like you do
that's why I seep motivation al into you
I use the pad as my catcher's mitt
as I throw strikes which surely stick
the sentences form through letters vow
arranging themselves the best they know how
I correct their positions when out of place
getting assurance through your face
as we intimately form the stage
for Slongentl to be uncaged

I'm Digging You

Into extreme nervousness each time your eyes meet mine
Making me nauseous but in a good way

Damn I'm digging you
It's like I want to be the nutrients in your vitamins
Giving you all from a to zinc
Gelatinizing all that's within
Into unquestionable love for you
Not lust its deeper than that
Giving my life if needed be

Your knight in the darndest of armor
Out shining the bravest and most handsome
Underlining my feelings right here in front of you

letting you know far down inside I'm Digging You

Stop

Stop undressing me with your eyes
That will only lead to us laying side by side

Stop telling me all the things you wanna do to me
It will only lead to us being naughty as can be

Stop making suggestions with that cucumber
It will only lead to me debarking the lumber

Stop imitating those sounds that them actresses make
It will only lead to us laying in a pool of our own lake

Stop touching me where I want to be touched
It will only lead to us both being blush

Stop…just stop this is not what I wanna do
I will only lead to me getting to know you

Getting to Know You

dinner for two at a secluded venue
movie accompanied by a foot massage from me to you
questions floating as molecules in the sky
is it wrong for me to like him like this…she's high
blushed as thy face caresses the softest Smiles
feelings catch up to the butterflies' miles
magnetic conversations intertwine yours with mine
attraction is inevitable
edible you are as we go through our sensual progression

Ever Could Be

composed melodies humanize as
the sunset paints itself
over the ocean's horizon
a smile slowly sprawl
across my face
as I discard it all
as she emerged
from the softest of wavs
I embraced the dream of us
slow dancing with the stars
under the tepid moonlight
exotic as it may sound
I don't even recall her noticing me
as she toweled
her chiseled physique
free from water
she turned slowly and
winked at me as my eyes
fixate on her upper thighs
distraught was I inside
for I wondered
If we
ever could be

Skate Night

as cologne and perfume mix
each smile compliments our performance
to cover our fronts in order
for our skates to shove us back
as if to lash our act
to the hardwood floor
embarrassed are we
as our clumsiness airs over the loudspeaker
so hot and sexy
even as we bust our derriere
trying to relive earlier times
as king and queen of skate night

If Eyes Could Talk

If eyes could talk
There would be no need for me
As you soak the essence of my stare
Slongently you are aware
Truthfully I will sensually take care
Of the very Incompetence you share
With that other one
You call honey bun
Even when you look at him
Seeing the other woman
Thy dreams cease with me
Within my retina's deliverance
Thy discover climax consistence
If eyes could talk
There would be no need for me
As you soak the essence of my stare
Slongently you are aware
Truthfully I will sensually take care
Of the very Incompetence you share

Ecstasy's Escapade

hoping wishing pondering
mental swindle bundle of nerves
consuming my abdomen
every thought reenacts visions of you
sexy erotic exotic
unveiling yourself
available for entry
gentleman like I oblige
a dream…a reality
realistically aiding you to new heights
yearning to take you there
patiently I partake in thee
as you thankfully take the whole of me
sweet Karma Sutra the aroma
this moment is as precious as the flowers on thy mantle
astonished as I concur our slowest of dance
your soft skin melts as each touch grasp thy apple curvature
each kiss as fine as the Merlot we sipped
as I sipped the essence of you
thy eyes close in seductions silence
heavenly embraces conclude ecstasy's escapade
may we lay together again…and again

Cozy Fire

come...the fires a blaze
soothingly gesturing thy near
sparkles glaze from the chandelier
ambiance set with music easy on the ears
the couch readies for you and I
to lie helpless in each other's arms
feeling the warmth from the flames
as the reflection flickers in thine eyes
I'm held captive inside
may I rise to put another piece on top
to heighten up the emotional spot
intimacy spilling from the two of us
the bold of us...
the juice...
the mold of us
smoldering inside our cozy fire

Blame it on the Alcohol

One hundred beers on body…
Or was it bottles of beer
Alcohol is totally speaking near
Creeping closer and closer till I asked her
What you drinking I will buy another
She replied fine as long as I can have you under covers
Come on tonight lets be sweet lovers
Gin on the rocks and hers straight as I rocked
Hard up as the tallest skyscraper
Laughing hysterically while she massaged it gently
Consequently
She Angelina
I'm digging every inch her demeanor
She grabbed my hand
Pulled me to her car
Drove me near not far
Up three flights of stairs
I'm fading in and out
Distant lights…solar flares
Between stretched eyeballs and casting glares
One more beer and I'm done for the night
As the lights dimmed I barely see her face
but felt her body every place
Can't believe its morning and there was a rude awakening
Blame it on the alcohol is time for this occasion

For the artist who sings this song
Played a character who I just broke out of her home
Screaming that Gina is her girl
She going to tell her that she rocked my world
Damn…it was Wanda…blame it on the alcohol!

Moist As The Tropic's Precipitation

time flies in quantum leaps
aftermath of love conjured beasts
appetite unmatched by any other
imprinted inside her
moist as the tropic's precipitation
sipping her nectar as the sun rises
gulping me down coating her horizon
freaky grin as she licks her lips
quick gasps of air as she spreads her hips
moans to screams
screams to pants
pants to silence
silence to waking to me still inside
creamy and oozing love's existence
for years to come
repeat our love's reminiscence
candlelight on the beach's bed
all night lovemaking
being constantly fed
her body spongelike
soaking up the whole of me
Massaging the length of me

Sombre Sweet Sunset

sombre sweet sunset
pinecone's scent inside my mind
cruising so slowly

eyes so beautiful
hair flows free as the willow tree
lips so seductive

we gaze at the sea
waves captivate our love's past
wind blows us away

cozy in the loft
as pups to a mother
we warm each other

in ways undescribed
firefly like inside I
illuminate her

until the morning
songbirds sing forever last
in my mind always

Heartbeats I Think…

intense pretense ends romance
hard earned in every way
motivation rages on
heartbeats I think…

hard earned in every way
proven pleasures branded hearsay
heart beats think…
I think once more deserved

proven pleasures branded hearsay
unappreciated never unintentional
I think once more deserved
Never ending vows not in our future

Propose

the question prosed
the answer proposed
aloft the dome of
paradox's home
innocence bare as the eagle
experience seeping with mixed signals
is it safe to feel your touch
want your lust
yearn for us
recycle the effects of love
experiment the aftershock
subconsciously atop the world
contemplating ejection
rejection
reconnection
flabbergasted at our alienation
our true identities revealed
naked as a blank canvas
we search ourselves for
the passwords that
set us free
alas
we unlock each other's treasures
with the words
will you…

Espouse

nausea affixed itself inside me
it had me at hello
long kiss goodnight cherished nevermore
my heart beats all but minus a few
the air is thin within
inner cherubim beckons us close
may we ignite under the holiest of hosts
starry eyed by the heavens above
none added humility
only beauty and dignity
I envision a lavish carriage
drawn by two beautiful stallions
cream in complexion
eyes filled with determination
anxiety overtakes nausea as we
approach our destination
the crowd stood shocked
as you stepped out
I followed right behind you
all of tradition has been cut loose
I held your train high for you
we journey across the field of daises
rice and rose petals fall willingly at our feet
we approach the river
we step in together

fixate upon each other as
the pastor reads God's words
I do… I do
we submerge
as I take her in my arms cradle style
we emerge
as I carry her
through the rain of petals and rice
to the boat waiting to carry us off down the river
as confetti fly us on into the horizon